A GIFT FOR:

Ginny

FROM:

Karen

X-Mas 2022

Copyright © 2017 Hallmark Licensing, LLC

Published by Hallmark Gift Books,
a division of Hallmark Cards, Inc.,
Kansas City, MO 64141
Visit us on the Web at Hallmark.com.

Editorial Director: Delia Berrigan
Editor: Kim Schworm Acosta
Art Director: Chris Opheim
Designer: Scott Swanson
Production Designer: Dan Horton

Contributing Writers: Joey Benevento,
Ellen Brenneman, Jake Gahr, Bill Gray,
Megan Haave, Jeannie Hund, Keion Jackson,
Tina Neidlein, Dan Taylor, Melissa Woo

ISBN:978-1-63059-720-7
1BOK1418

Made in China
1221

PET PRAYERS

FUNNY PLEAS AND PRAISE FROM OUR ANIMAL FRIENDS

DEAR GOD,
PLEASE HELP!
THEY'RE EXERCISING
ME AGAIN, AND YOU
KNOW I'M NOT
MADE FOR IT.
AMEN.

NOW I LAY ME DOWN TO SNORE,
UPON MY DOG BED ON THE FLOOR,
UNTIL YOU FALL ASLEEP, AND THEN,
I'LL JUMP UP ON YOUR BED AGAIN.

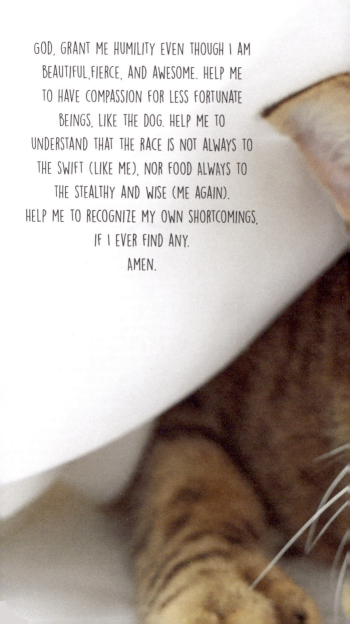

GOD, GRANT ME HUMILITY EVEN THOUGH I AM
BEAUTIFUL, FIERCE, AND AWESOME. HELP ME
TO HAVE COMPASSION FOR LESS FORTUNATE
BEINGS, LIKE THE DOG. HELP ME TO
UNDERSTAND THAT THE RACE IS NOT ALWAYS TO
THE SWIFT (LIKE ME), NOR FOOD ALWAYS TO
THE STEALTHY AND WISE (ME AGAIN).
HELP ME TO RECOGNIZE MY OWN SHORTCOMINGS,
IF I EVER FIND ANY.
AMEN.

DEAR GOD,
PLEASE ALLOW MY OWNERS
THE WISDOM TO KNOW THOSE
AREN'T CHOCOLATE SPRINKLES
I LEFT BEHIND.

DEAR GOD,
THANK YOU FOR
MAKING ME SO PRETTY
THAT IT REALLY DOESN'T
MATTER IF I'M SMART.
AMEN.

DEAR LORD,
PLEASE HELP MY HUMAN
TO UNDERSTAND THAT THIS YELLOW
THING ISN'T AN ACTUAL DUCK.
NO FEATHERS, NO BILL, NO QUACK.
RETRIEVERS HAVE PRIDE, YOU KNOW.
AMEN.

LORD, I PRAY THAT I AM THE GOOD BOY
MY HUMAN IS TALKING ABOUT WHEN SHE SAYS
"WHO'S A GOOD BOY?"
I *THINK* I'M A GOOD BOY, BUT SHE ASKS OVER
AND OVER AND OVER AGAIN, SO I JUST
CAN'T BE SURE. I MEAN, IS THERE ANOTHER
GOOD BOY, AND AM I SUPPOSED TO KNOW HIM?
BECAUSE I DON'T BELIEVE WE'VE MET.
IT'S CONFUSING, LORD.

LORD, BLESS THIS FOOD I'M ABOUT
TO TURN MY NOSE UP AT.

DEAR LORD,
WE DON'T ASK MUCH . . .
ONLY THAT YOU SMITE THE CAT.
AMEN.

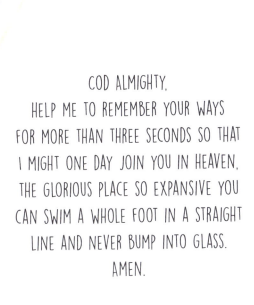

COD ALMIGHTY,
HELP ME TO REMEMBER YOUR WAYS
FOR MORE THAN THREE SECONDS SO THAT
I MIGHT ONE DAY JOIN YOU IN HEAVEN,
THE GLORIOUS PLACE SO EXPANSIVE YOU
CAN SWIM A WHOLE FOOT IN A STRAIGHT
LINE AND NEVER BUMP INTO GLASS.
AMEN.

GOD, GRANT ME THE SERENITY
TO ACCEPT THE THINGS I SHOULD NOT CHEW.
ENTHUSIASM TO CHEW THE THINGS I CAN,
AND WISDOM TO KNOW THE DIFFERENCE.
AMEN.

LORD CREATOR, IN YOUR LOVE,
YOU HAVE MADE THE FINCH AND DOVE,
BROUGHT FORTH SPARROWS, BLACKBIRDS, BATS,
HAMSTERS, GERBILS, MICE, AND RATS,
SPIDERS, BEETLES, CRICKETS, SLUGS,
BUTTERFLIES, AND LADYBUGS,
LIZARDS, RABBITS, FROGS, AND FISHES.

THANK YOU, LORD.
THEY'RE ALL DELICIOUS.

NOW I LAY ME DOWN TO SLEEP,
I PRAY THE LORD MY MASTER TO BRING
HOME 'CUZ I'M FREAKING OUT HERE
HE'S BEEN GONE FOR 14 MINUTES
I JUST WANNA KNOW IF HE'S OK
AND I'M REALLY SORRY BUT I'M IN
NO STATE TO COME UP WITH
RHYMING PRAYERS RIGHT NOW.

TO HELP ME WASH OFF
ALL MY DROOL,
DEAR GOD,
PLEASE SEND A BIGGER POOL.

LORD, I THANK YOU FOR MY WRINKLY
FACE, CHUBBY BODY, AND STUBBY LEGS —
AND ESPECIALLY FOR YUMMY THINGS
LOW TO THE GROUND.

LORD WHO PARTED THE SEA,
WHO WALKED ACROSS THE WAVES,
WHO FLOODED THE EARTH,
WHO CAUSED WATER TO BURST
FORTH FROM THE ROCK,
PLEASE HELP ME HOLD IT IN
UNTIL IT'S TIME FOR MY WALK.
HOUSE—TRAINING IS SO DANG HARD,
BUT WITH YOU, ALL THINGS ARE POSSIBLE.

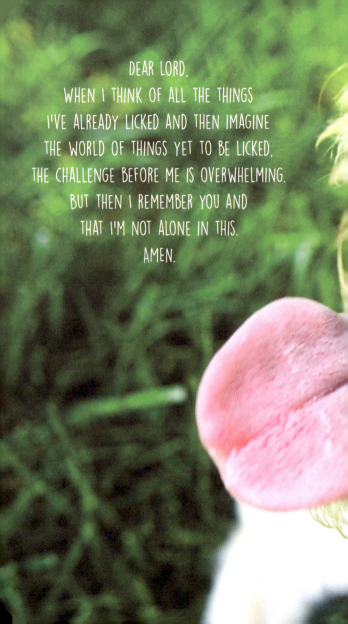

DEAR LORD,
WHEN I THINK OF ALL THE THINGS
I'VE ALREADY LICKED AND THEN IMAGINE
THE WORLD OF THINGS YET TO BE LICKED,
THE CHALLENGE BEFORE ME IS OVERWHELMING.
BUT THEN I REMEMBER YOU AND
THAT I'M NOT ALONE IN THIS.

AMEN.

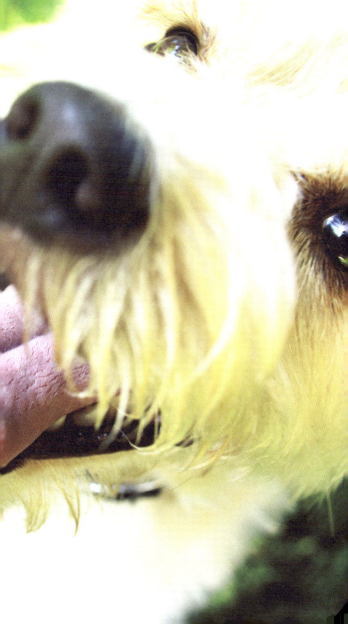

I THANK YOU, LORD,
THAT I CAN POUNCE,
AND JUMP AND BOUND AND LEAP . . .
AND LAND UPON THE
UNSUSPECTING
HUMANS AS THEY SLEEP.

LORD, PLEASE HELP MY HUMAN.
TODAY, HE TOOK A PERFECTLY NICE TENNIS BALL
AND THREW IT ACROSS THE YARD. HE STARTED
ACTING ALL RESTLESS, SO I PICKED IT UP
AND BROUGHT IT BACK. HE SEEMED SO HAPPY.
BUT THEN SUDDENLY HE THREW THE BALL AGAIN!
I DON'T KNOW WHAT HE WANTS.
GIVE ME THE UNDERSTANDING TO HELP HIM.

BLESS THE CLEAN-MAKERS,
FOR THEY REMOVE WHATEVER IT IS I ROLLED IN.
PROTECT THEM FROM SPRAY WHEN I SHAKE MYSELF,
AS WE ALL KNOW I MUST, AND KEEP ME FROM
UNFLATTERING HAIRCUTS, SINCE I DO NOT MAKE
THAT CALL, YET I AM THE ONE WHO SUFFERS.
AMEN.

LORD, HELP ME TO WALK IN YOUR FOOTSTEPS
WAIT—DID SOMEONE SAY "WALK"???

BLESS MY COMING IN AND MY GOING OUT;
VERILY, THERE IS NO REASON FOR EITHER.
HELP ME TO RUN FULL ON OUT THE DOOR,
ONLY TO RETURN IN ONE MINUTE, WITHOUT
SO MUCH AS A STICK. PROTECT ME AS I FACE
THE UNCERTAIN OUTDOORS, AND THANK YOU
FOR THE COMFORT THAT WAITS INSIDE.
AMEN.

DEAR LORD, THANK YOU
FOR THE BLESSING OF MY CHILDREN.
ALL TWENTY SEVEN OF THEM.
OH DEAR, HERE THEY COME NOW.
GUESS THAT'S "AMEN" THEN.

LORD, IN YOUR INFINITE WISDOM,
YOU CREATED ALL GOOD THINGS:
SQUIRRELS TO CHASE, PEANUT BUTTER TO EAT,
CROTCHES TO SNIFF . . . BUT IN MY IMPERFECT
CANINE UNDERSTANDING, I HAVE TO ASK WHY
YOU CREATED THE VACUUM. PLEASE ENLIGHTEN . . .
OH NO HERE IT COMES NONONO HELP!!!

PLEASE SEND STEW MEAT FROM LAST NIGHT
OR PIZZA CRUSTS WOULD BE ALRIGHT,
A JUICY RIB WOULD BE DELISH
OR BACON CRUMBLES IN MY DISH!
PERHAPS A TASTY CHICKEN LEG?

**THIS DOGGIE AIN'T
TOO PROUD TO BEG!**

PLEASE GUIDE ME WHILE I SEARCH THE TRASH
TO DIG AROUND, THEN DINE AND DASH.
DON'T CARE IF SNACKIN' MAKES ME SICK—Y . . .
BRING IT, LORD, 'CAUSE I AIN'T PICKY!

LORD ON HIGH,
BEFORE YOU FORMED ME IN THE EGG,
YOU KNEW ME. IN YOUR WISDOM,
YOU GAVE ME A SAFE AND PLEASANT CAGE.
BUT, SEEING I WAS LONELY, YOU TOOK
FROM ME A WISHBONE AS I SLEPT
AND FORMED A HEN TO BE MY COMPANION.
THANK YOU FOR HER MUSICAL SQUAWK
AND HER GRACEFUL FLAPPING.
AMEN.

LORD,
PLEASE HELP.
THE HUMANS HAVE
DONE IT AGAIN.
AMEN.

NOW I LAY ME DOWN TO REST
SO I CAN DO MY VERY BEST
AT CATCHING MOUSES WHEN I RISES
('CAUSE MY HUMANS *LOVE* SURPRISES).

UM, HI, GOD?
SORRY TO BOTHER YOU.
I KNOW YOU'RE SUPER BUSY
BUT I HAVE A FAVOR TO ASK.
UM . . . COULD YOU SEND, LIKE,
A LITTLE OIL FOR MY HAMSTER WHEEL?
JUST A DROP?
THE SQUEAKING IS KINDA DRIVING
ME *OUT OF MY FREAKIN'* . . . ER,
I MEAN, THY WILL BE DONE.
AMEN.

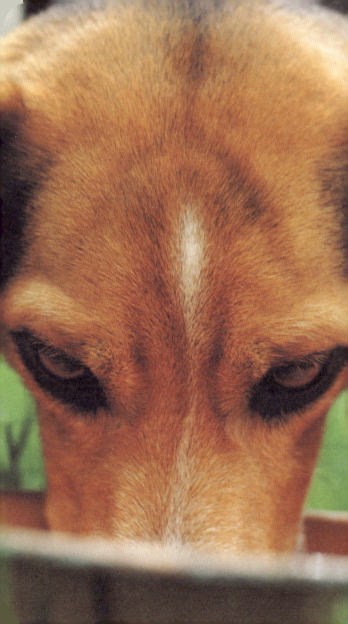

LORD, THANK YOU FOR THIS FOOD,
PROVIDED BY YOUR BOUNTY
AND THE MIRACLE OF THE
ALL—POWERFUL CAN OPENER.

DEAR LORD,
FORGIVE US OUR TRESPASSES . . .
IN THE GARDEN, ON THE COUCH,
ON THE BED, IN THE TOILET,
ON THE DINNER TABLE,
IN THE CAT'S BOWL,
AND IN THE GARBAGE.
AND PLEASE LET THEM CONTINUE
TO BUY OUR "SORRY" ACT SO
THEY CAN'T STAY MAD.
AMEN.

HELP ME, LORD,
TO LOVE MY NEIGHBOR—
EVEN THIS ONE NEXT TO ME
WITH REALLY BAD BREATH.

FORGIVE ME, LORD,
FOR I HAVE SINNED.

ONCE ON THE STAIRS
AND ONCE ON THE RUG.

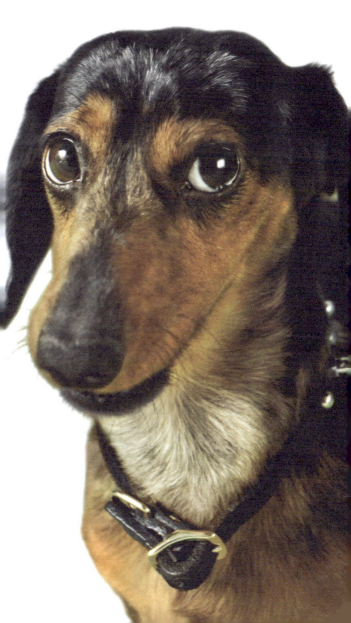

DEAR LORD,
I PURR IN YOUR HONOR.
AND I DON'T PURR FOR
JUST ANYONE,
YOU KNOW.

DEAR GOD, THANK YOU FOR
TOO MANY BLESSINGS TO COUNT!
EXCEPT CHOCOLATE, WHICH, OF COURSE,
IS TOXIC AND PUT HERE SO THAT WE
CAN LEARN RESTRAINT AND IN SOME
WAY UNDERSTAND HOW ADAM AND EVE
FELT WITH THE APPLE.
AMEN.

LEAD ME NOT INTO POISON IVY, AND
DELIVER ME FROM OTHER DOGS,
LEST I SNIFF THEM INAPPROPRIATELY.
HELP ME TO BE OBEDIENT, WHILE
REMAINING TRUE TO MY ANIMAL NATURE.
FOR THINE IS THE FRONT YARD,
THE SIDEWALK, AND THE WHOLE
BLOCK, FOREVER.
AMEN.

SORRY, OH LORD, THAT I SHARE
EASTER WITH YOUR SON.
IT WASN'T MY CHOICE.

CLEARLY, I DON'T ALWAYS KNOW
WHAT'S BEST FOR ME.
PROTECT ME FROM MYSELF—MY
URGES, MY DESIRES, MY TENDENCY
TOWARD SELF-DEFEATING BEHAVIOR.
LET WISDOM BE MY GUIDE,
EVEN IF IT HAS TO BE ENFORCED
BY A PLASTIC CONE OF SHAME.
AMEN.

TODAY
WE LIFT OUR VOICES
UP TO YOU.
AND THE UPS GUY.
AND SQUIRRELS.
BUT MOSTLY YOU.

AS WE EMBARK ON THIS FEARSOME
AND MYSTERIOUS JOURNEY,
THE FINAL DESTINATION OF WHICH CAN
NEVER BE KNOWN 'TIL WE GET THERE,
AND THEN NEVER REMEMBERED,
PLEASE GIVE US PATIENCE WITH EACH OTHER.
ESPECIALLY IF ONE OF US SEES
A CAT OUTSIDE THE WINDOW.

DEAR GOD, PLEASE LET ME GROW BIG AND MEAN SO I CAN PROTECT
THEM. AREN'T I DUE FOR WHAT THEY CALL A "GROWTH SPURT"?
NOW WOULD BE FINE!
I'VE BEEN PRACTICING MY MENACING STARE AND DEEP, SCARY BARK.
WOULDN'T I LOVE TO SEE THE MAILMAN BACK AWAY IN TERROR
AND THE WOULD—BE BURGLAR CROSS THE STREET IN FEAR?
YIP! YIP! . . . I MEAN GRRRRR.

GOD, I THANK YOU,
FOR I AM FUR—FULLY
AND WONDERFULLY MADE.

IF YOU ENJOYED THIS BOOK
OR IT TOUCHED YOUR LIFE IN SOME WAY,
WE WOULD LOVE TO HEAR FROM YOU.

PLEASE WRITE A REVIEW AT HALLMARK.COM,
E-MAIL US AT BOOKNOTES@HALLMARK.COM,
OR SEND YOUR COMMENTS TO:

HALLMARK BOOK FEEDBACK
P.O. BOX 419034
MAIL DROP 100
KANSAS CITY, MO 64141